Acknowledgements

I would like to thank Dr. Carolyn Stevenson, Dr. Kareem Muhammad, Dr. Farid Muhammad, Victor Powell of Powell photography, my family, friends and all the barbershop conversations that sparked a lot of the humorous topics for my poems. Also I would like to thank that special lady, she knows who she is. Thank you for purchasing Poetry is Dead. I was inspired to write many of the poems in this book, based from personal life changing experiences. In October 2009, I was inspired to begin a nonprofit organization, The Project Tiers Foundation in Chicago, Illinois. Project Tiers Foundation addresses the violence in the urban communities, with mentoring teenagers and giving them positive options in life along with furthering their educational options. For more information, please contact me at **info@pjtiers.org**

Table of Contents

Twenty

Forty-five and aged to perfection

I'm sure twenty-five years ago

Her curves would have given me sexual

Erections

Matured mentally

My harassments are of the purest nature.

Spiritually we connect with the heavens

Emotionally the tides secure our love

Off-shore

Romantically our minds

Intertwine with divine sexuality.

Forty-five and my love for

Her is true and pure.

Her tears, shadows

The cursed sadness of her beautiful eyes

She's ashamed of thirty-five

It's too late, my love has changed,

Age and time has troubled her heart

I refuse to let twenty years keep us apart.

Socks

Corn is for soup and a Bunion for Paula

Spare my eyes from the horrid sight

Your toes and feet

Seemed to have been in a fight.

Lotions and oils sold to the local stores

By the fleet; do me a favor

COVER YOUR UGLY ASS FEET!

Island Girl

Black, brown, beautiful, and bold tales

About aggressive love.

Her smile reveals teeth

As white as a dove's tail.

Her ebony eyes.

Pursue a passionate, sexual stare.

I realize the strength and beauty,

Of her locked hair.

Her heavenly body

Firm as steel, the Earth

Unveils her sex appeal Island girl.

Lonely Rock

Lonely rock stranded, and

Covered in sand.

Let me give you a hand!

One toss and a skip

Now you are among friends.

1%

Not again, you caught your man in bed

With his best friend.

Now you have opened the flood gates

To find Dennis and his

Friend are soul mates.

What a terrible blow to your self-esteem

Loose the homogenized ..... Man

And let me plant seeds

Of an organic man

Who will never stray away.

From your grassy pastures

And get lost in some man's rapture.

I enjoy my rule of life

Only a woman can be my wife

So I stay away from

The rides at every man-land.

Even locked away

I will never go astray

I will use both of my hands to tend

To my own farmland

Years have passed.

And I am back in your arms

We rock the barn yard from front to back

So the next time you catch

Your homogenized man in the act; call me

and I will keep you glued on your back,

Without mountains being broken.

African Queen

Black coffee no sugar, hold the cream

Please stir with your finger

And let the sweetness linger.

Delicate skin, ripened from God's sun

Mother has blessed your nature

Sexually repressed you are

I promise my tongue

Will not oppress your body.

Our love will free us

Into sexual revolution

My African Queen has climaxed to sexual

Evolution.

Gravy

Spicy rice is nice but where are the beans to

Accompany my rice?

Red, black, or navy

Skip the legumes they cause pong fumes

I'll have my chicken with gravy.

Free Eyes

Winter whips against the discoloring, aging

Rock.

The salt settles

On top of the black rock

The moon takes its place

Behind the third cloud.

The sun rises with perfection

As the temperature of the heat settles with

The wind, colorful,

Birds are chirping in perfect harmony.

Yoga has calmed the young lady's
Emotional stress,
Winter is far and spring has left with the
Rains.
The young lady's ears record the years that
Have passed.
Nature's familiar creatures
Always fill my empty thoughts
I wonder why the world has free eyes.

Painful Love

Love produces pain and mental strain.

Unconditional love reduces pain and eases

Psychological strain.

After the knife was removed from my back

The dark room whispered

A lover's theme my sinful blood stained

The satin sheets.

Her love invited death.

Where's The Beef?

What happened to the music?

Stolen jazz drums, borrowed soul rhythms

Hard rock 'n' roll made me stroll

To the other side of music.

Dark killers,

Pill poppers,

Women beaters,

Bi-sexual Gemini's,

Gun transporters, drug dealers

And homosexual ass fillers.

The disturbed talentless voices.

Rattles my musical intelligence

Into a purple haze of confusion.

Is he a woman or is she a man?

I ask where's the beef?

Gone forever.

The west coast became vegans,

The east coast became choir boys,

The dirty south became clean,

And the Midwest floated downstream.

Today the artist inject un-pure musical

Notes

Like dope fiends.

Tainted their bloodstream with

Commercialism.

Blood no longer red like an apple

Today real music is being sampled.

Black Beauty

Black Beauty, powerful 5.0 engine

Black leather seats, soft as a lamb ass

Sleek body built for racing.

Triple black paint skinny's the muscle

The real beauty

Is on someone's ranch

I'm just twenty-one and ranch life

Is for a settled man

With a wife and two kids.

Patience comes with forty

And married life comes with strife the

Mustang. I drive is for city life.

Rain

Heavens and gray clouds

Produce distant rains

I imagine roller-skating

Looking through my window pane.

The sun shadows the neighborhood

I turn to unlock the door

Step outside and the clouds

Hide the sun, why does nature play

Ruin my day?

A Colored Rose

Blue rose, blue as the heavenly skies

White rose, white as the clouds above

Green rose, green as Eden's garden

Red rose, red as the fiery pits of hell

Black rose, black as the devils skies of

Night

Yellow rose, yellow as God's beautiful sun

A polluted rose turns pale

My eyes are color blind

And not for sale.

Opposites Attract

Happiness, Sadness, Love, and Hate

Are the opposites

Of my life.

Empty Rooms

A large bracket for the wealthy

A lower bracket for the unhealthy

The poor may never afford tennis rackets

Only round balls and higher taxes.

The lower class takes

All the economical down falls and every

Now and then

Attend an inaugural ball.

Lights, camera, action

The governor has an addiction

For power and fame, finger pointing and

Shame.

Scandalous corruption in city hall

The mayor won't even take the blame.

So the Olympics invent a new game

Where's the president?

The colorless house in D.C

Have new residents.

Peace

Knowledge is wisdom to build kingdoms

Religion provides faith and wars promote

Hate.

Organized police enforce peace

While innocent men are forced in cages

Without Miranda rights.

The powerful kingdom has been crushed

To an invisible height

The wounds reveal

A horrid sight from the war.

Religious faiths provide spiritual guidance

For peace and freedom. Something you

Only encounter

When you are deceased **PEACE!**

Summer In Chicago

Sunglasses to filter out the UV rays

Sweat meeting with every gland of your

Body

Not even interested with the summer

Hotties.

Just a drink of water to keep

You out the city morgue

One bottle for a dollar

At the corner store.

The air conditioner provides a subtle cool

Freeze

The store clerk smiles a fox grin

Once he closes the store.

He too will bend from the

Sun's hot wind

Summer time in Chicago.

Divine

The hourglass is turned upside down

Sensual lovemaking becomes a sport

Begging for mercy

Pleasuring for love.

My mind controlling

Invades her passionate intimate thoughts

Her body is a map of heavenly sins

My tongue is featured as a navigation tool

Her breast sit divine like two ripe mangos.

Her ebony hair nestled behind her ears

Lips delicate and mature

For a lovers war invasion,

Imperfections of her perfect body

Reveals the beauty marks on her stomach.

Her knees bend and her back is arched,

As my tongue invades her volcano

Hot lava begins to flow.

As my tongue is being shuffled back and

Forth

Like a deck of cards

My tongue elevates her ass

One inch off the bed.

My ears become her steering wheel

Her direction unknown

Her melodic tones become silent

My debut at the opera

Has erupted her volcano

With my tongue exercise.

Omega Man

The winds howl and the trees grow 100 feet

Tall

Forbidden treasures

Of the earth run free.

Flowers bloom, the land is plentiful

With buzzing bees, birds chirping, and

The wolf is howling at the murky moon.

The clouds lay tucked behind the lost stars

The sun becomes lost in darkness

Smog and smoke choke the organic land

Buildings submerge under sea levels

Of contaminated water.

I search for clean water

To quench my thirst

One oak tree to provide shade

As a cool breeze whispers freedom to my

Enslaved ears.

One man me-and one woman somewhere

Lost.

She is out there; my guess begins with her

Mother,

Planet earth lost somewhere

Between the moon and stars

I wonder if she is too far

To create a love child

To deliver to the heavens.

Years have passed and my search is over

Our daughter created the last man standing.

In Tune

Passion, Emotion, searching for

The right word

That has meaning.

Loud theatrics

Mystifying word play

Slams the poet

Salty tears, stain the cheeks

Multiple lovers have stained the sheets

Inspired for the love of words

Two lovers in tune with the melodic beat.

Cargo

Ships are docked

The cargo bruised and beaten.

Cuba got half the cargo

Brazil got five Nubian queens.

America got 100 bucks; not dollars

But men made of green

To fulfill the devil's greed.

Ironed collars choked the necks

Steel shackles bruised the wrists

It is off to the market

To be sold as merchandise.

100 niggers to be precise

Free today and bought tomorrow

The handcuffs today only bring sorrow

Free your mind and your ass shall follow

Out of bondage forever.

Bullshit

Words, Meaning, Slam,

Spoken word

Rapping, Poetry, Literature.

Good and band theories

Equals bullshit

Poetry is dead.

Interlude To A Romance

Romance is not an act

Romance is an emotional act

Romance is not flowers

Romance is not happiness

Romance is not peace

Romance is not an interruption of feelings

Romance is not love

Romance is dead.

Music Man

Tears of a clown smears the makeup

Beauty is only skin deep

Proud Mary carries a band of gold

He's gone forever, so there is only one egg

left to fry.

Big girls don't cry

Maybe we should give love another try

And roll with the stones of love

Me and Mrs. Jones.

Jazz

Hip Hop Boom, the snares fill the room

Tip Tap Toom, the bass fills the room

Dip Dap Doom, the piano chords fill the

Room.

La La La her voice shrinks the room.

Wiz Waz Waz I'm jazz in your eardrum.

Love Potion #9

One drop to clear the eyes

Another drop to poison the heart

Four drops for pure passionate sex

Three drops to make her mine

Measured correctly to equal nine.

Too many drops and true love will be blind

Love potion number **9**.

Rum

Rum is strong and dark

Rum is light and sweet

Rum is good with a coke

But too much rum can make you choke.

Rum is great when baked in cakes

Rum is good for sorrow

Don't drink too fast and please savor

A glass for tomorrow.

Weeks have passed And you've had a ton

Of Rum

Especially in your colada.

Too much Rum made you forget the Pina

Now you're in bed with a man named Ted

Dressed as Tina!!!!!!

Breathe Mint

Beautiful hair short and croppy

Put together very well never sloppy.

Eyes excited with Jade

Skin as ebony as God's dark skies

A tight borrowed ass from her mother

And perfect breast passed down from her

Grandmother.

Our eyes have met once or twice in a

Lighted room

The perfection of her body is in tune

And aligned with my Jupiter moon

Her foul breath

Ruined my sexual mood

So why are we nude in my room?

Paying respects to her Venus moon.

I offered her a mint

So my nose may feel content

Next year I'll make her my wife.

First impressions are not everything

Now she can enjoy a mint diamond ring

Every time we do the wild thing.

Memories

Holidays fill the room with laughter

Cameras flash to store the memories

Forever

Happiness overshadows the gloom;

The keys open the doors

To the empty rooms.

I sit and wait by the window

As the moonlight peaks off the lake

My soul realizes

I am not awake. My spirit

Waits for daybreak

That's when I make my journey across the

Lake.

My family mourns over my tombstone

Every Memorial Day in May, and maybe

An occasional family holiday.

The pictures restore my physical being

When sadness approaches their hearts

My spirit walks through the

Empty rooms as I approach the dark.

As a beam of light keeps us apart.

Seven years have passed and at times they

Forget me and our past.

I wonder if they or anyone truly

Remembers.

I shall know when life

Invites death in December.

Black Russians

Russia's dark skies and bitter cold

Along with two much vodka and tales of

Old

My caramel complexion blends well with

Russian snow bunnies.

A drunken night filled with white Russians

Black beauties conceal their curvaceous

Bodies

With white sables

The beauties are twins.

With cold charcoal eye's and devilish grins.

The white vodka condemns me

To a night of sin.

My friends embark on the same journey to

Russia

And ask the bartender

For black Russians and make them twins.

The Morning After

I love you whispered in my ear.

Passionate biting and trembling love

Shakes.

Screams of ecstasy along with

X-rated fantasies; I control my mechanics

From the bottom

Because if on top her nectar from nature

Would have made me pop.

Our love comes to a complete stop

I forgot to take my pill

Was whispered in my ear.

What did I have to fear?

Maybe some infectious disease

Please we were monogamous

Nine months later I whispered to my

Daughter

I love you dear.

Protest

Crazy world

Crazy him

Crazy you

Crazy her

Animals for food

And crazy me

Because I like furs.

Savage

Dead man.

Alive man.

Dead man.

Lively man.

Proud man.

Humble man.

Big man, little man, Greedy man, big heart

The last man ripped it out.

Sexual Conversation

Her eyes undressed my soul

My passion for her dangles

For sexual pleasure, as she veto's

My sexual temptations.

I wangle her into full submission

As I am her vice Roy

To her sovereign body.

My tongue understands

Her vagina monologue. My sexual dialogue

Never said I loved her.

Wonderful Thoughts

Thoughts only reveal deeper thoughts.

My thoughts conceal my personal thoughts,

I only have memories of my most

Profound thoughts.

Kite

Fly high kite

Fly with the gusty winds

Please Mr. Wind

Don't bend the pole to my kite!

One snap and my kite

Is out of sight.

The colors are really bright!!

Religion

Allah said it's a way of life

Jesus said you must repent your sins

And Jehovah has returned.

I didn't get the memo

From God!!

I must have overslept.

Autumn

Brown

Red

And autumn leaves

Cold filtered rain though semi dark skies.

This is my time of year

To think and drink

An autumn beer.

The right amount of hops and barley

Gives you the best brew

Enjoyed with jalapeno cornbread and lamb
Stew.
Sometimes I wish the summer and winter
Would stall so I can enjoy the indefinite
Images of fall.

Black And Brown All Over

A masters plan to control the land

A wonderful plan to enslave a man,

A devious plan to torture a Godly woman.

A jealous man who betrayed his king

Now his people look to the heavens and

Sing.

A tainted hand to curse a man!

The creator's master plan to leave his sheep

With a permanent tan.

Spirit World

You open your arms and embrace me

You accept me for what I used to be

Now a speckle of light

Your distant memories are gone out of

Sight.

I remember the sun and moon

And how your love was my cocoon.

The tears I shed bought gloom and your

Memories made new flowers bloom,

Along with sunlight and heavy rains.

I know my leaving

Caused you so much pain

Grieve not for me.

My spirit is never in vain

Listen to the birds, raindrops, and the two

Songs

That reminds you of me

On your iPod

I left this atmosphere to be with my God.

Answer Me

Why did he do it?

I don't know maybe to be

Accepted and not rejected by his peers.

Not being cool is one of his fears

Or maybe because he believes he is tough

And being a gangster

Was the only education.

He was taught That nigga should have put

His hands up and fought.

Hell a bullet to the back of his head

Was his first thought

Why did he do it?

He doesn't know

Caged in time; his consciousness will grow.

Words

Slicing painful words

Sharp angry words

Beautiful words

Loving words

Too many damn words,

My tongue fell off.

Falling

One step forward

Six steps backwards

Eight steps to the left

Three steps to the right

I'm falling beneath the earth.

Health Care

What a scare!!!!!

There is health care in Cuba

And life is free in France.

Health care belongs to the people for a

Price

So roll the dice

Your roll of lucky seven was missed.

So why gamble with your health!!

Only in America do you need

Wealth for health care to exist!!

A Letter To My Children

Happiness when I heard you cry

What a joy to be

Replicated in my image.

Created in love your innocence

Became my guilt

Praying I am the best man for the job

Too late!

For all the thoughtless wonderings

And second guessing

I belong to you forever

I will guide you and shield your innocence

Protect your pride

And discipline you when needed.

And never turn my back on you

You belong to the world now

And that my beautiful children

I cannot protect you from.

Hot Chocolate

Smooth, buttery cocoa……..

Warm to the touch

Steam peeking over the rim of the mug.

Delicate blowing so I do not interrupt

The whip cream from her thighs

She giggles waiting for me to indulge

In her chocolate volcano.

Her back arches as I savor every drop

Chocolate morsels erupt as I lick the rim

Of the Chocolate pot

It's fun when I hit the Chocolate spot.

White Russians

Cold piercing topaz eyes

Cheek bones sturdy

As mountain tops, legs of cold steel.

She arrives at my door naked

In a black Sable fur coat

My eyes connect with her perfectly shaved

Peach

Unusual…. It's too cold to grow peaches in

Russia.

Her black suede heels add three inches

To her curvaceous body

And twelve inches to my sexual arousal

Pints of vodka

Sipped from her navel

My stamina compromised from the Russian

Vodka.

I awoke the next morning with two white

Russians.

Bedroom Eyes

Eyes that pierce the soul and look deep

Within my spirit.

Our eyes connect with pure intimate

Thoughts

Of sexual pleasure.

I pleasure myself with virgin thoughts

Of bedroom fantasies

Welcome to sin city

Your bedroom eyes satisfy my sexual

Imagination

Her bedroom eyes are sexual stimulation.

Wind

Howling screeching wind

Makes my knees bend

Stop blowing in my ear disastrous wind.

Tree

One hundred years and you are still

Standing

Bark is smooth as Amber.

Molasses seeping from your branches

Money green leaves and a shade of sixty

Degrees.

Then you were struck by lightening

And died.

When I got the bill for the stump removal

I cried.

Hopeful

Tower

Key

Peace

Lock

Watch me shock the world.

Humble Pie

Flaky crust

Blueberry filling

Apple pie is America's beginning

A humble life is fulfilling.

Chess

A **Knight** captures a rook

A **King** is a crook

A **Bishop** studies the book

A **Pawn** is out on the look

A **Queen** is off the hook

Check mate

I captured the **SPOOK**!

The Boxer

Mr. William's son loves to box

Mr. William's boxing moves resemble a

Fox

Mr. William's son claims kingdom

As King of the block.

Mr. William's son won't study to be a

Chip off the old rock

Mr. William's opponents are unable to

Block.

Mr. William's opponent is left dazed and
Shocked from the brutal hand and technical
Body shots.
One day Mr. William's opponent won't be
Lady
Mr. William's ideas of boxing a man would
Be crazy.

The Ark

Young and gifted with spiritual insights

A pen and pad to capture

Your most prophesized moments.

Rational people protest a Sooth-Sayer to

The highest claims

A catastrophic rain destroyed the writings

Who shall know of your fame?

Sharpie & Sign

Will work for food

Will work for shelter

Can you help me?

Third Eye

Tonight the moon is murk from the

Spiritual eye

Divine sun disables darkness,

While the world continues to rotate.

Traveled light will elevate the

Consciousness.

Caged

The man with the key
Should be encaged.

Trust

To trust me is to know me

So why should I trust you?

Especially when we don't know each other.

Let's learn to trust one another

And trust love will forget

Our trust in each other to love.

Lost Summers

We closed the door to our hearts in the

Spring

We used to laugh

And be blissful together.

Late nights cuddled under

The fireplace during winters

Now our love drifts

With the autumn winds.

I beg the summer to mend our love as

Friends.

The Gift & The Curse

At times I revel in the time

We spend together. Profound

Memories and deep conversation

As I master her heavenly body and

Beautiful mind.

She is a gift to my soul

When our moments together are put on

Hold.

She pushes for our physical to fritter more
Often
She spoils the moments we integrate
Our love.
Heavens gift from above
Is what our physical will transcend to
Unconditional love.

The Birth

The screams deliver joy

To a mother and father.

Ten toes

Ten fingers

Perfection bound

With high expectations

To get through life.

Sin

Beauty assembles love

Love resembles hate

Hate harbors peace

Ugly despised beauty

And sin is pure

Holiness is life's cure.

One Sided

One love blossoms

One love transcends

One love plays possum

One love sometimes bends

One love is swift

One love is pure

One love is a gift

One love is sure

One love is painful

Our love makes me grateful.

Quest

Munificent gatherings are memories lost

From yesterday

Infused with a scorned heart

For tomorrow.

Questioning love or reasoning

With love taints the discovery of love

Test of Relentless bargaining for loves

Honesty

And loyalty only leads

To a lonely quest.

One would consider love

Should be natural

To the eye and poisonous to the heart

A love quest should never keep

Our love apart.

Ass-Sets

Ms. Jackson represents the emblematic

Of the mother-land, when Ms. Jackson

Walks her heavily construction, causes

Massive destruction to traffic.

Ms. Jackson treasure orchestrates the

Rhythm of tribal drum, Ms. Jackson

Has musical buns.

Local

Sweet juicy Florida oranges,

Juicy delicious crisp Michigan apples,

Sweet ripe Georgia peaches,

Divine Mexican Mangos,

And a Honduran melon,

Sold at a local Chicago Store.

Fried Shrimp

Scavenger of the ocean,

Caught in a fishermen's trap,

Pulled aboard and dumped onto

The vessel floor

Destination unknown

Frozen on a bed of ice

Waiting to go to a distant home

To be peeled, deveined, and

Dredged in Old Bay seasoning.

Panko crumbs, fried to perfection,

And accompanied with cocktail sauce.

Peta would suggest I'm a wimp

My appetite must be fulfilled with a fried

Shrimp.

Red Line

A stench of urine, a baby convoluted

Screams

And an out of control teen

Talking loudly on a cell phone.

A drunken bum delights in

Teasing my five senses

This beats pushing your horn

And road rage

This train needs a crazy cage.

Next stop 95th!

www.ingramcontent.com/pod-product-compliance
Lightning Source LLC
Chambersburg PA
CBHW071234090426
42736CB00014B/3079